crafting a new nation

The Story of Betsy Ross For Kids

sarah michaels

contents

introduction

Betsy Ross wasn't always the famous figure we know today. She started her life as an ordinary girl, born into a large Quaker family in Philadelphia on January 1, 1752. From a young age, Betsy was known for her creativity and skill with her hands. She learned how to sew and stitch from her great-aunt, and these skills would become a huge part of her life.

Philadelphia, where Betsy grew up, was a bustling city even in those days. It was a place of commerce and culture, filled with people from all walks of life. Betsy's family lived in a simple Quaker household, where hard work and simplicity were valued. Quakers were known for their plain dress and straightforward way of living, and these values shaped Betsy's character. Even as a child, Betsy was hardworking and determined, qualities that would serve her well in the years to come.

Betsy loved spending time in her father's shop, watching him work as a carpenter and learning about different materials and tools. She was curious and always eager to help. When she was old enough, Betsy was sent to a Quaker school, where she learned reading, writing, and arithmetic. But it was her needlework that truly set her apart. She had a natural talent for sewing, and she enjoyed creating beautiful things from simple pieces of fabric.

As Betsy grew older, she became an apprentice to a local upholsterer, learning to make and repair household items like curtains, bedcovers, and furniture. This apprenticeship was a big step for Betsy. It was here that she met a young man named John Ross, another apprentice who shared her passion for craftsmanship. Betsy and John fell in love and decided to get married, even though it meant leaving the Quaker community, as Quakers did not approve of marrying outside their faith.

Married life was both joyful and challenging for Betsy and John. They started their own upholstery business in Philadelphia, working side by side to build a life together. They were happy, but their happiness was short-lived. The Revolutionary War broke out, and life in the colonies changed dramatically. John joined the local militia to fight for American independence, leaving Betsy to manage the business on her own.

The war brought many hardships to Betsy's life. Supplies were scarce, and many of her friends and family were affected by the conflict. Despite these challenges, Betsy continued to work hard, using her skills to support herself and contribute to the war effort. It was during this difficult time that Betsy's story took a historic turn.

Legend has it that in June 1776, Betsy Ross received a visit from three important men: George Washington, Robert Morris, and George Ross, her late husband's uncle. They came with a special request that would change her life forever. They asked Betsy to create a flag for the new nation they were fighting to build. According to the story, Betsy suggested some changes to the design, including making the stars five-pointed instead of six, because they were easier to sew. The men agreed, and Betsy set to work.

Creating the first American flag was no simple task. Betsy carefully chose the materials, cutting and stitching with precision and care. She knew this flag would represent the hopes and dreams of a new nation, and she wanted it to be perfect. The result was a beautiful flag with thirteen red and white stripes and thirteen white stars on a blue field, representing the original thirteen colonies.

When the flag was finished, it was presented to the Continental Congress, and it quickly became a symbol of American independence and unity. The sight of the flag inspired soldiers and citizens alike, giving them hope and a sense of pride in their new country. Betsy Ross's contribution to the American Revolution was more than just a piece of fabric; it was a powerful emblem of freedom and resilience.

But Betsy's story doesn't end with the creation of the flag. She continued to work as an upholsterer, supporting herself and her family through her craft. She married twice more, first to Joseph Ashburn, a sailor who was captured and died in a British prison, and then to John Claypoole, a fellow patriot and old friend. Together, Betsy and John raised their children and continued to live in Philadelphia.

Betsy Ross lived a long and full life, passing away in 1836 at the age of 84. Her legacy, however, lives on. The story of her role in creating the first American flag has been passed down through generations, making her a beloved figure in American history. While some details of the story have been debated by historians, there is no doubt that Betsy Ross's skills and spirit were a significant part of the nation's early years.

Today, Betsy Ross's house in Philadelphia is a museum, where visitors can learn about her life and see where she created the first flag. The American flag she helped design continues to be a powerful symbol of the United States, representing the ideals of liberty, justice, and unity.

why betsy ross matters

To understand why Betsy Ross matters, we need to think about the time in which she lived. The late 1700s was a period of great change and upheaval. The American colonies were fighting for their independence from British rule, and there was a strong sense of urgency and determination among the people. Everyone was trying to do their part to support the cause of freedom, and Betsy Ross was no different.

Betsy's creation of the first American flag was a significant moment in history. At a time when the new nation was struggling to define itself, the flag provided a powerful symbol of unity and identity. Imagine being a soldier in the Revolutionary War, fighting in harsh conditions, far from home. Seeing the American flag flying high would have been a source of inspiration and hope, a reminder of what they were fighting for. This symbol, stitched together by Betsy Ross, helped to unite the colonies and gave people a common emblem to rally around.

But Betsy's importance goes beyond the flag itself. Her story is one of perseverance and resilience. Life was not easy for Betsy. She faced many challenges, including the loss of her husband and the difficulties of running a business during wartime. Yet, she never gave up. She continued to work hard, using her skills to support herself and her family. This determination is a key reason why Betsy Ross matters. She showed that even in the face of adversity, it is possible to make a meaningful contribution.

Betsy Ross's legacy also highlights the importance of ordinary people in shaping history. Often, we hear about famous leaders and big battles, but it's the everyday actions of individuals like Betsy that truly make a difference. Her story reminds us that everyone has a role to play, no matter how small it may seem. By doing her part and using her talents, Betsy Ross helped to create a lasting symbol of American freedom and independence.

In addition, Betsy Ross's story is a testament to

the power of creativity. The flag she created was not just a piece of cloth; it was a work of art that represented the ideals of a new nation. Her ability to take a simple idea and turn it into something beautiful and meaningful is a powerful lesson. It shows that creativity and innovation are essential qualities, not just in times of peace, but especially in times of struggle.

Moreover, Betsy Ross is an important figure because she broke barriers. In a time when women's roles were largely confined to the home, Betsy was a businesswoman and a skilled artisan. She took on a task that had national significance and excelled at it. Her story encourages us to challenge traditional roles and pursue our passions, no matter the obstacles.

Betsy's work also had a lasting impact on the perception of the American flag. Over time, the flag has come to represent not just the original thirteen colonies, but the values of liberty, justice, and unity. Every time we see the American flag, we are reminded of the principles on which the country was founded. Betsy Ross's flag is a symbol that continues to inspire and bring people together, reinforcing the idea that the United States is a nation built on shared ideals and collective effort.

Another reason why Betsy Ross matters is that

her story is a source of inspiration for future generations. Learning about Betsy and her contributions helps young people understand the importance of dedication and hard work. It teaches them that even in difficult times, it's possible to achieve great things through perseverance and creativity. Betsy's life is a powerful example of how one person can make a difference, and her story continues to motivate and inspire people today.

Furthermore, Betsy Ross's legacy is a reminder of the importance of recognizing and celebrating the contributions of women in history. For many years, the roles of women in shaping history were often overlooked or minimized. By learning about Betsy Ross and her achievements, we gain a more complete understanding of the past and acknowledge the vital contributions of women. Her story encourages us to appreciate and honor the diverse individuals who have played a part in shaping our world.

Betsy Ross's impact is also evident in the way her story has been preserved and celebrated. Her house in Philadelphia has been turned into a museum, attracting visitors from all over the world. People come to learn about her life, see where she lived and worked, and gain a deeper appreciation for her contributions. The museum serves as a testament to Betsy's enduring legacy and ensures that her story continues to be shared with future generations.

In addition to her role in history, Betsy Ross has become a symbol of American values. The qualities she embodied—hard work, creativity, resilience, and patriotism—are still highly valued today. Her story reminds us of the importance of these values and encourages us to strive to uphold them in our own lives. Betsy Ross is not just a historical figure; she is a role model whose life and work continue to resonate with people of all ages.

Betsy Ross's contributions also highlight the interconnectedness of the American Revolution. Her work on the flag was part of a larger effort by many individuals to achieve independence and build a new nation. Understanding her story helps us appreciate the collective effort and collaboration that went into the founding of the United States. It reminds us that great achievements are often the result of many people working together toward a common goal.

1 /
early life

birth and family

PHILADELPHIA in the 18th century was a lively place. It was one of the largest cities in the American colonies, and it was growing rapidly. The streets were often crowded with merchants, craftsmen, and people from all walks of life. Betsy's father, Samuel Griscom, was a skilled carpenter and builder. He worked hard to provide for his large family, constructing houses and doing various woodworking projects around the city. Rebecca, Betsy's mother, managed the household, which was no small feat with so many children to care for.

Life in the Griscom household was busy and structured. The family followed Quaker principles, which emphasized simplicity, hard work, and honesty. The Quakers, also known as the Religious Society of Friends, were known for their plain dress and their commitment to equality and peace. These values were instilled in Betsy from a young age and would shape her character throughout her life.

Growing up in a large family had its challenges, but it also meant that there was never a dull moment. Betsy was surrounded by siblings, and there was always someone to play with or help out with chores. The Griscom children were expected to contribute to the household from a young age. Betsy, like her siblings, learned to help with cooking, cleaning, and other daily tasks. But it wasn't all work and no play. There were also plenty of opportunities for fun and games, and the Griscom children made the most of their time together.

One of Betsy's favorite activities was watching her father work in his carpentry shop. She was fascinated by the way he could take simple pieces of wood and turn them into beautiful, functional items. Samuel Griscom was not just a builder; he was also an artist in his own right. His skill and craftsmanship were well respected in the community, and Betsy admired his dedication to his work.

It was in this environment of creativity and hard work that Betsy developed her own talents. From a young age, she showed a natural aptitude for needlework. Under the guidance of her great-aunt Sarah Elizabeth Ann Griscom, Betsy learned to sew and stitch. She quickly became skilled with a needle and thread, and her work was admired for its precision and beauty. Needlework was an important skill for girls at that time, and it was one that would prove invaluable to Betsy in her later years.

Education was also an important part of Betsy's upbringing. The Griscom children attended a Quaker school, where they learned reading, writing, and arithmetic. The Quakers believed in the value of education for both boys and girls, which was not always the case in other communities. At school, Betsy developed a love for learning that stayed with her throughout her life. She was curious and eager to absorb new knowledge, whether it was about history, geography, or practical skills like sewing.

The Quaker school also taught values like honesty, integrity, and compassion. These principles were reinforced at home by Samuel and Rebecca. The Griscom family regularly attended Quaker meetings, where they participated in silent worship and listened to the teachings of their faith. These experiences helped to shape Betsy's moral compass and gave her a strong sense of right and wrong.

As Betsy grew older, her responsibilities in the household increased. She took on more significant tasks, helping her mother with cooking and caring for her younger siblings. These experiences taught her valuable lessons in responsibility and time management. They also strengthened the bond between Betsy and her family members. The Griscom household was a close-knit unit, and the support and love they shared helped them navigate the challenges of daily life.

Despite the demands of household chores and her education, Betsy always found time for her needlework. She would sit by the window in the evenings, using the fading light to finish her latest project. Her stitches were tiny and even, and she took great pride in her work. It was clear to everyone that Betsy had a special talent, and her family encouraged her to pursue it.

When Betsy reached her teenage years, she was ready to put her skills to use in a more formal setting. At the age of 21, she became an apprentice to an upholsterer named William Webster. This was a significant step for Betsy, as it allowed her to refine her skills and learn new techniques. Apprenticeships were a common way for young people to learn a trade during this time, and it provided Betsy with valuable hands-on experience.

Working with William Webster, Betsy learned to make and repair a variety of household items, including curtains, bedcovers, and furniture upholstery. She quickly became known for her attention to detail and her ability to produce high-quality work. Her reputation as a skilled seamstress grew, and she began to receive commissions from prominent families in Philadelphia.

It was during her apprenticeship that Betsy met John Ross, a fellow apprentice who worked in the same shop. John was charming and kind, and the two quickly became close. Despite their different religious backgrounds—John was an Anglican and Betsy a Quaker—their bond grew stronger, and they eventually decided to marry. This decision was not without its challenges. Marrying outside the Quaker faith meant that Betsy would be expelled from the Quaker community. However, her love for John was strong, and she chose to follow her heart.

On November 4, 1773, Betsy and John eloped, marrying in New Jersey because they could not be married in a Quaker meeting house. The newlyweds returned to Philadelphia and started their own upholstery business. They worked together, combining their skills and talents to build a successful enterprise. Life was good for the young couple, but their happiness was soon interrupted by the outbreak of the Revolutionary War.

quaker roots

Betsy Ross's upbringing in a Quaker family played a significant role in shaping who she was and what she stood for. The Quakers, or the Religious Society of Friends, were a unique group with strong values that influenced every aspect of their lives. Living in the Griscom household, Betsy was immersed in these principles from the day she was born, and they helped mold her character and guide her actions throughout her life.

Quakers believed in simplicity, peace, integrity, community, equality, and stewardship. These core values were not just ideas but were woven into the fabric of daily life. For the Griscom family, simplicity meant living without excess. Their home was modest and their clothes plain, reflecting their belief that outward appearances should not distract from one's inner virtues. Betsy grew up wearing simple dresses without fancy lace or frills, learning early on that what mattered most was not how you looked, but how you treated others.

Peace was another fundamental Quaker principle. Quakers were known for their pacifist beliefs and their commitment to resolving conflicts without violence. This value was particularly important during Betsy's lifetime, as the American colonies were often embroiled in conflicts and eventually the Revolutionary War. In the Griscom household, the idea of peace extended beyond just avoiding physical confrontation. It included fostering a peaceful and harmonious environment at home and within the community. Betsy learned to approach problems with a calm and thoughtful demeanor, a trait that would serve her well in both her personal and professional life.

Integrity and honesty were highly valued in the Quaker community. Quakers believed that one's word should be as good as a written contract. This meant that lying, cheating, or any form of dishonesty was strictly against their principles. Growing up, Betsy was taught the importance of being truthful and keeping her promises. Whether she was helping with household chores or completing a sewing project, she knew that doing her best and being honest about her efforts were crucial.

Community and helping others were central to the Quaker way of life. The Griscom family was part of a close-knit Quaker community where members supported each other through thick and thin. This sense of belonging and mutual aid was comforting and empowering. Betsy often saw her parents and other community members come together to help those in need, whether it was through providing food, shelter, or emotional support. These experiences instilled in her a deep sense of compassion and a desire to contribute positively to society.

Equality was another cornerstone of Quaker beliefs. Unlike many other groups of the time, Quakers believed in the equality of all people, regardless of gender, race, or social status. This was a radical idea in the 18th century, a time when women and people of color had very few rights. In the Griscom household, everyone's voice was heard, and both boys and girls were encouraged to pursue education and develop their talents. Betsy grew up knowing that she was just as capable and valuable as anyone else, which gave her the confidence to take on challenges and make her mark in history.

Stewardship, or taking care of the world and its resources, was also a key value for Quakers. The Griscom family believed in using resources wisely and taking care of their environment. This meant not being wasteful and making the most out of what they had. Betsy learned to be resourceful and innovative, skills that would prove invaluable in her work as an upholsterer and flag maker. She understood the importance of sustainability long before it became a common concept.

Betsy's education was another important aspect of her Quaker upbringing. The Quakers valued education for both boys and girls, which was not always the case in other communities during that time. Betsy attended a Quaker school where she learned to read, write, and do arithmetic. These skills were essential for her future business endeavors and personal development. The school also reinforced the values she learned at home, creating a consistent and supportive environment for her growth.

The Quaker practice of silent worship was a unique and profound part of Betsy's spiritual life. Quaker meetings involved sitting together in silence, waiting for the inner light or divine guidance to speak to them. This practice encouraged introspection and a deep connection to one's inner self. For Betsy, these moments of quiet reflection were an opportunity to center herself and find clarity. This inner peace and connection to her faith provided a steady foundation throughout her life's ups and downs.

Another aspect of Quaker life that influenced Betsy was the community's emphasis on service. Quakers believed in actively working to improve society, whether through social justice efforts, charitable work, or simply being kind and helpful to others. Betsy saw this service-minded approach in action every day, from her parents helping neighbors to larger community projects aimed at aiding the less fortunate. This instilled in her a lifelong commitment to service and a desire to use her skills to make a positive impact.

Living by these Quaker values was not always easy. The Griscom family, like other Quakers, faced challenges and opposition, especially during times of conflict. Their pacifist stance was often misunderstood, and their refusal to swear oaths or participate in certain governmental practices set them apart. Despite these challenges, the Griscoms remained steadfast in their beliefs, teaching Betsy the importance of standing up for what you believe in, even when it's difficult.

As Betsy grew older and faced her own challenges, the values instilled in her by her Quaker upbringing continued to guide her. Her commitment to simplicity, honesty, and integrity was evident in her work and interactions with others. Her belief in equality and community support helped her navigate the complexities of life in a diverse and rapidly changing society. And her dedication to peace and stewardship influenced how she approached problems and found solutions.

2 /
growing up

childhood adventures

ONE OF THE most exciting parts of Betsy's childhood was her time spent exploring Philadelphia. In the mid-1700s, Philadelphia was one of the largest cities in the American colonies. The streets were alive with the sounds of merchants selling their goods, horses trotting by, and children playing. Betsy loved to wander these streets, always with a sibling or two by her side. The city was a place of endless fascination for a curious young girl. She would watch blacksmiths at their forges, marvel at the ships docked at the port, and listen to the lively conversations of people from all walks of life.

One particular adventure that stood out in Betsy's memory was her visits to the bustling market. The market was a colorful and noisy place, filled with vendors selling everything from fresh produce to handmade goods. Betsy enjoyed accompanying her mother on trips to the market, helping to select the best fruits and vegetables for their family. She loved the smell of fresh bread and the sight of vibrant fabrics being sold by merchants. These trips were not just about shopping; they were also a chance for Betsy to learn about the world around her and the importance of community and trade.

At home, Betsy's adventures often took the form of learning new skills. One of her favorite activities was working alongside her father in his carpentry shop. Samuel Griscom was a skilled carpenter, and he enjoyed teaching his children about his trade. Betsy was particularly fascinated by the tools and techniques he used to create beautiful pieces of furniture. She would watch intently as he planed wood, hammered nails, and crafted intricate designs. Her father's patience and attention to detail made a lasting impression on Betsy, and she took great pride in helping him with small tasks.

Another important aspect of Betsy's childhood was her education. Attending a Quaker school, Betsy learned reading, writing, and arithmetic, but the lessons extended far beyond the classroom. The Quaker values of simplicity, honesty, and equality were woven into every aspect of her education. Betsy and her classmates were encouraged to think critically, ask questions, and engage in discussions. This environment fostered a love of learning that stayed with Betsy throughout her life.

One memorable educational adventure involved a school project on the natural world. Betsy and her classmates were tasked with creating a detailed map of their neighborhood, highlighting important landmarks and natural features. This project required them to explore their surroundings, observe the world with fresh eyes, and work together as a team. Betsy enjoyed this project immensely, relishing the opportunity to combine her artistic skills with her curiosity about the environment. The finished map was a testament to their hard work and collaboration, and it was proudly displayed in the school for all to see.

Betsy's adventures weren't limited to structured activities. She also had plenty of time for play and imagination. One of her favorite pastimes was playing games with her siblings in the spacious yard behind their house. They would invent elaborate stories and act them out, transforming their yard into a magical world of knights, castles, and hidden treasures. Betsy often took on the role of the storyteller, using her vivid imagination to create exciting plots and characters. These games were not only fun but also helped Betsy develop her creativity and storytelling abilities.

Wintertime brought a different kind of adventure. When the first snowfall blanketed Philadelphia, Betsy and her siblings would bundle up in warm clothes and rush outside to play in the snow. They built snowmen, had snowball fights, and went sledding down the nearest hill. The crisp air and the joy of playing in the snow made these winter days some of Betsy's favorite childhood memories. Even the chores, like bringing in firewood or helping to clear the snow, felt like part of the fun.

Another adventure that Betsy cherished was her time spent with her great-aunt Sarah Elizabeth Ann Griscom, who was a talented seamstress. Aunt Sarah recognized Betsy's interest in needlework and took her under her wing, teaching her the intricacies of sewing and stitching. Betsy's lessons with Aunt Sarah were both educational and enjoyable.

She learned how to make precise stitches, create patterns, and choose the right fabrics for different projects. These sessions were filled with stories and laughter, and they ignited a lifelong passion for needlework in Betsy.

Betsy's childhood was also shaped by the Quaker meetings she attended with her family. These meetings were a time for quiet reflection and community worship. For a young Betsy, sitting in silence for long periods could be challenging, but she grew to appreciate the sense of peace and contemplation it brought. During these meetings, she would listen to the adults speak about their faith and the importance of living a life of integrity and service. These gatherings reinforced the values she learned at home and school, helping to shape her moral and ethical beliefs.

One particular Quaker meeting left a lasting impression on Betsy. A traveling Quaker minister visited their meeting house and spoke passionately about the importance of peace and justice. His words resonated deeply with Betsy, and she felt inspired to live by those principles. This experience strengthened her commitment to the Quaker values of pacifism and equality, guiding her actions and decisions throughout her life.

As Betsy grew older, her adventures began to

take on new forms. She started to take on more responsibilities at home, helping her mother with cooking, cleaning, and caring for her younger siblings. These tasks were not always easy, but they taught Betsy important lessons about responsibility and cooperation. She learned to work efficiently and to take pride in her contributions to the household.

One of Betsy's most significant childhood adventures was learning to run her own small business. Encouraged by her parents, she began to take on sewing projects for neighbors and friends. She made and mended clothes, created household items like curtains and bedcovers, and even designed her own patterns. This early experience in entrepreneurship taught Betsy valuable skills in customer service, time management, and financial planning. It also gave her a sense of independence and confidence in her abilities.

learning a trade

Aunt Sarah was known for her impeccable needlework, and she was more than happy to pass on her knowledge to young Betsy. Their lessons were not just about sewing; they were moments of bonding and storytelling. Aunt Sarah would often share stories about their family history or tales of the city, making each sewing session an adventure of its own. Betsy was an eager student, always ready to learn new stitches and techniques. Her small hands would carefully mimic Aunt Sarah's movements, practicing until her work was just as neat and precise.

The skills Betsy learned from Aunt Sarah were the foundation of her trade. She mastered the basics of sewing: threading a needle, making various stitches, and finishing edges. But her lessons didn't stop there. Aunt Sarah also taught her how to repair clothes, create patterns, and select the right materials for different projects. These were valuable skills that would serve Betsy well in her future endeavors.

As Betsy grew older, her interest in needlework continued to blossom. Her family recognized her talent and encouraged her to pursue it further. At the age of 21, Betsy became an apprentice to an upholsterer named William Webster. This apprenticeship was a significant step in her journey, providing her with formal training and hands-on experience in a professional setting.

Working with William Webster, Betsy learned the intricacies of upholstery. This was a craft that required a combination of precision, strength, and creativity. Upholsterers were responsible for making and repairing household items like chairs, sofas, curtains, and bedcovers. Betsy learned how to work with different fabrics, measure and cut materials accurately, and use various tools to assemble and finish pieces. Each project was a new challenge, requiring attention to detail and a steady hand.

One of the first tasks Betsy learned was how to create patterns for upholstery. This involved measuring the furniture piece accurately and then designing a pattern that would fit perfectly. Betsy's mathematical skills, honed during her Quaker schooling, were put to good use here. She had to ensure that every piece of fabric was cut precisely to avoid wastage and ensure a snug fit. This required not just technical skill but also an understanding of the materials and how they behaved.

Another important skill Betsy acquired was tufting, a technique used to secure the fabric to the furniture frame with buttons. This added both a decorative element and durability to the upholstered piece. Tufting required precision and strength, as Betsy had to pull the fabric tight and secure it in place without causing any wrinkles or damage. She practiced this technique diligently, knowing that the quality of her work would reflect on her reputation as a craftsperson.

Betsy also learned about the importance of selecting the right materials for each project. Different fabrics had different properties; some were more durable, while others were more decorative. Betsy had to understand the needs of her clients and choose materials that would meet those needs while also staying within their budget. This aspect of her training taught her not only about the materials themselves but also about customer service and the importance of listening to her clients' preferences and requirements.

One memorable project during her apprenticeship involved creating a set of drapes for a wealthy family in Philadelphia. This was a prestigious commission, and Betsy was determined to prove her skills. She selected a rich, heavy fabric that would provide both privacy and insulation. The drapes needed to be meticulously measured and sewn, with pleats and hems finished to perfection. Betsy worked long hours on this project, applying everything she had learned from Aunt Sarah and William Webster. When the drapes were finally installed, they transformed the room, adding an air of elegance and sophistication. The clients were thrilled, and Betsy's reputation as a talented upholsterer grew.

While Betsy was busy learning and perfecting her trade, she also formed strong bonds with her fellow apprentices. They shared tips and tricks, supported each other through challenging projects, and celebrated each other's successes. This camaraderie made the long hours more enjoyable and provided a sense of community and belonging. These relationships were important to Betsy, as they offered both professional support and personal friendship.

Betsy's apprenticeship also included learning how to run a business. William Webster was not just a skilled upholsterer; he was also a savvy businessman. He taught Betsy how to manage orders, keep track of supplies, handle payments, and interact with clients. These lessons were invaluable, as they prepared her for the day when she would run her own business. Betsy took these lessons to heart, understanding that her success as an upholsterer would depend not just on her technical skills but also on her ability to manage her business effectively.

Outside of her formal training, Betsy continued to practice and refine her skills at home. She often took on small projects for family and friends, creating and mending clothes, making decorative items, and even designing new pieces of furniture. These projects allowed her to experiment with different techniques and styles, further developing her creativity and innovation. Betsy's family was proud of her work and supported her efforts, providing a constant source of encouragement and motivation.

3 /
the young
seamstress

betsy's apprenticeship

BETSY STARTED her apprenticeship in the bustling shop of William Webster, a well-known upholsterer in Philadelphia. The shop was a lively place, filled with rolls of fabric, spools of thread, and various tools for sewing and upholstery. The air was often filled with the sounds of scissors snipping, needles piercing fabric, and the murmur of conversations between apprentices and customers.

From the very beginning, Betsy threw herself into her work. She quickly discovered that being an apprentice wasn't just about sewing; it was about understanding the entire process of creating beautiful and functional items. Her day would typically start early in the morning, helping to open the shop and prepare for the day's work. She would sweep the floors, organize materials, and make sure everything was in its place.

One of the first skills Betsy had to master was cutting fabric. This may sound simple, but it required precision and care. The fabric had to be measured accurately and cut cleanly to ensure that the final product would fit perfectly. Betsy learned to use large, sharp scissors, handling them with the confidence of a seasoned craftsperson. Each snip of the scissors was deliberate, as any mistake could mean wasting valuable material.

Next, Betsy learned the various types of stitches and when to use them. There were simple running stitches for basic seams, sturdy backstitches for strength, and delicate whipstitches for finishing edges. Each type of stitch had its purpose, and Betsy practiced them until she could execute each one flawlessly. She spent hours perfecting her stitches, her fingers nimble and quick as she worked the needle and thread through the fabric.

One memorable project involved reupholstering a set of dining chairs for a local family. The chairs had seen better days, with worn-out fabric and sagging seats. Betsy, under the guidance of William Webster, took on the task with enthusiasm. She carefully removed the old fabric, taking note of how the chair was originally assembled. Then, she measured and cut new fabric, choosing a durable yet attractive material that would breathe new life into the chairs.

Reupholstering the chairs was a complex process that required multiple steps. Betsy started by attaching new padding to the seats, ensuring they were comfortable and supportive. Then, she meticulously stretched the new fabric over the frames, securing it with tiny, even stitches. The final touch was adding decorative trim, which not only hid the seams but also added an elegant finishing touch. When the chairs were completed, the transformation was stunning, and the clients were delighted with the results.

Betsy's apprenticeship also taught her the importance of customer service. She learned how to interact with clients, understanding their needs and preferences. William Webster emphasized the importance of listening to customers and providing them with personalized service. Betsy found that she enjoyed these interactions, taking pride in helping clients choose the right fabrics and designs for their homes.

One day, a wealthy merchant came into the shop with a special request. He wanted a set of custom-made curtains for his grand parlor, a room where he often entertained important guests. The curtains needed to be both functional and decorative, providing privacy while also enhancing the room's elegance. Betsy was excited to take on this project, seeing it as an opportunity to showcase her growing skills.

The process began with a visit to the merchant's home, where Betsy measured the large windows and discussed the desired look and feel of the curtains. Back at the shop, she carefully selected a luxurious fabric in a deep, rich color. She then set to work measuring, cutting, and sewing the fabric into panels. Each panel needed to be exactly the right length and width, with perfectly even hems and seams.

To add a touch of sophistication, Betsy decided to incorporate pleats into the design. Pleating required careful folding and stitching, and it added both texture and volume to the curtains. The finished product was stunning, with the pleats creating elegant waves that cascaded down to the floor. When the curtains were installed in the merchant's parlor, they transformed the room, adding a sense of grandeur and refinement.

Throughout her apprenticeship, Betsy faced numerous challenges, but she always approached them with determination and a willingness to learn. One particularly difficult project involved repairing a damaged set of tapestries. The tapestries were old and fragile, with intricate designs that required meticulous care. Betsy spent hours carefully mending the tears and reinforcing the weakened areas, using her skills to preserve the beauty and integrity of the artwork.

Working on the tapestries taught Betsy the importance of patience and attention to detail. Every stitch mattered, and there was no room for haste or carelessness. The experience also deepened her appreciation for the artistry and craftsmanship involved in her trade. She realized that her work was not just about making things; it was about creating pieces that would bring joy and beauty to people's lives.

As Betsy honed her skills, she also developed a keen eye for design. She began experimenting with different patterns and techniques, pushing the boundaries of traditional upholstery. One of her favorite projects was creating a set of embroidered cushions for a local family. She designed a floral pattern, drawing inspiration from the gardens she often admired in Philadelphia. Each cushion was a work of art, with vibrant flowers and leaves stitched in intricate detail.

Betsy's creativity and innovation did not go

unnoticed. Word of her talent spread, and she began receiving commissions from prominent families in Philadelphia. Her reputation as a skilled and imaginative upholsterer grew, and she took pride in knowing that her work was appreciated and admired.

Throughout her apprenticeship, Betsy formed strong bonds with her fellow apprentices. They supported each other through the challenges of their training, sharing tips and techniques, and celebrating each other's successes. These friendships provided a sense of camaraderie and community, making the long hours and hard work more enjoyable.

Betsy's apprenticeship was a time of growth and transformation. She entered the workshop as a young woman with a passion for needlework and emerged as a skilled and confident craftsperson. Her experiences during this period laid the foundation for her future career, equipping her with the skills, knowledge, and determination needed to succeed in a competitive trade.

meeting john ross

John Ross was also an apprentice upholsterer, learning the trade under a different master. Like

Betsy, he spent his days honing his skills, cutting and sewing fabric, and transforming ordinary materials into beautiful, functional items. John was known for his friendly demeanor and his knack for making even the most tedious tasks seem enjoyable. His cheerful attitude and quick wit made him popular among his peers.

Betsy first met John at a local market where artisans and craftsmen often gathered to purchase supplies. The market was a lively place, filled with vendors selling everything from bolts of fabric to the finest sewing needles. Betsy was browsing through a selection of materials when she noticed John examining a particularly vibrant piece of cloth. Their eyes met, and John flashed a warm smile.

"Looking for something special?" he asked, his eyes twinkling with curiosity.

Betsy returned the smile. "Just trying to find the perfect fabric for a new project," she replied. "It's for a set of drapes, and it needs to be just right."

John nodded appreciatively. "I understand the feeling. Every project deserves the best materials. I'm John Ross, by the way."

"Betsy Griscom," she introduced herself, extending her hand. They shook hands, and from that moment, a friendship began to blossom.

Over the next few weeks, Betsy and John found themselves crossing paths frequently, both at the market and in the bustling streets of Philadelphia. They discovered they had much in common, from their passion for upholstery to their shared values of hard work and creativity. Their conversations ranged from the latest trends in fabric to their dreams for the future. Betsy admired John's dedication to his craft and his positive outlook on life. He, in turn, was impressed by her skill and determination.

As their friendship deepened, John began to visit Betsy at William Webster's workshop. He would often drop by with a bundle of supplies or to share a new technique he had learned. These visits became the highlight of Betsy's day. She looked forward to their lively discussions and the way John's laughter could brighten even the dreariest afternoon.

One crisp autumn day, John invited Betsy for a walk along the banks of the Delaware River. The trees were ablaze with red and gold, and the air was filled with the earthy scent of fallen leaves. As they strolled along the riverbank, John spoke of his dreams of opening his own upholstery shop one day. He talked about the kind of business he wanted to run, one that prioritized quality and customer satisfaction.

Betsy listened intently, her heart swelling with admiration. "I believe you can do it, John," she said earnestly. "You have the talent and the vision. I have no doubt you'll be successful."

John smiled at her words, his eyes softening. "Thank you, Betsy. Your belief in me means a lot. And I have to say, I couldn't imagine a better partner in this dream than you."

Betsy's heart skipped a beat. She felt a warm blush spread across her cheeks. "I'd be honored to be part of your dream," she replied softly.

Their relationship continued to grow, and it wasn't long before they realized that their feelings for each other went beyond friendship. They shared their hopes, fears, and everything in between, finding comfort and strength in each other's company. John admired Betsy's resilience and creativity, while Betsy was drawn to John's kindness and unwavering optimism.

As their love blossomed, they faced a significant challenge: Betsy was a Quaker, and John was an Anglican. Marrying outside the Quaker faith meant that Betsy would be disowned by the Quaker community, a decision that weighed heavily on her heart. She loved her family and her faith, but she also knew that her love for John was something truly special.

One evening, as they sat together in Betsy's family home, John took her hand and looked into her eyes. "Betsy, I know this decision is not easy for you. I don't want you to feel like you have to choose between your faith and our love."

Betsy squeezed his hand, her eyes filled with determination. "John, my love for you is strong, and I believe that we can face any challenge together. I want to build a life with you, even if it means making difficult choices."

With her family's support, Betsy made the brave decision to marry John. On November 4, 1773, they eloped, crossing the Delaware River to New Jersey to avoid the disapproval of the Quaker community. It was a simple but heartfelt ceremony, attended by a few close friends who understood the depth of their love.

After the wedding, Betsy and John returned to Philadelphia, eager to start their new life together. They rented a small house and set up their own upholstery business, combining their skills and passion to create beautiful and high-quality products. Their shop quickly gained a reputation for excellence, and they found themselves with a steady stream of customers.

Running a business together was both challenging and rewarding. There were long hours and hard work, but there were also moments of joy and accomplishment. Betsy and John supported each other through every obstacle, their love growing stronger with each passing day. They celebrated their successes and learned from their failures, always striving to improve and innovate.

One of their most memorable projects was creating a set of upholstered chairs for a prominent Philadelphia family. The chairs needed to be both elegant and comfortable, a true showcase of their craftsmanship. Betsy and John worked tirelessly, selecting the finest fabrics, designing intricate patterns, and ensuring that every detail was perfect. When the chairs were finally delivered, the clients were overjoyed, and their glowing praise brought a sense of pride and satisfaction to Betsy and John.

As they settled into married life, Betsy and John dreamed of expanding their business and starting a family. They often talked about their future, imagining a life filled with love, laughter, and the fulfillment of their shared dreams. Their home became a haven of creativity and warmth, a place where they could be themselves and support each other in every endeavor.

Tragically, their time together was cut short. In 1776, just three years after their marriage, John Ross passed away suddenly. Betsy was devastated by the loss of her beloved husband, her heart heavy with grief. But even in her darkest moments, she found strength in the love they had shared and the memories they had created together.

4 /

a time of change

life in philadelphia

DAILY LIFE in Philadelphia was a mix of routine activities and the constant undercurrent of war. For Betsy, each day began early. She would rise with the sun, her small home filled with the first light of morning. The day started with simple chores—sweeping the floors, tending to the fire, and preparing a modest breakfast. Her home, like many others, was a place of both work and living, with her upholstery workshop just a few steps away.

Once the morning chores were done, Betsy turned her attention to her business. The workshop was a cozy space filled with rolls of fabric, spools of thread, and various tools. The rhythmic sound of her needle piercing the fabric provided a comforting routine amidst the chaos of the outside world. Betsy took pride in her work, whether she was repairing a piece of furniture or creating new draperies for a client. Each stitch was a small act of defiance against the uncertainty of the times, a way to maintain a sense of normalcy and purpose.

The streets outside her workshop were alive with activity. Vendors called out their wares, offering everything from fresh produce to hand-forged tools. Betsy often needed to venture out to purchase supplies, weaving her way through the crowded market stalls. The market was a micro-cosm of the city, bustling with people from all walks of life. There were farmers with their carts of vegetables, craftsmen showcasing their goods, and housewives haggling for the best prices. The mix of accents and languages reflected the diverse popula-tion of Philadelphia, a melting pot of cultures and ideas.

As she navigated the market, Betsy would sometimes encounter friends and neighbors. Conversations often turned to the latest news from the front lines or the decisions made by the Conti-nental Congress. The mood in the city was a mix of hope and anxiety. People were united by a common cause, but the constant threat of British attack loomed over them. Despite the fear, there was also a sense of determination and solidarity. The citizens of Philadelphia were committed to the fight for independence, each contributing in their own way.

One of the most striking aspects of life in Philadelphia during the Revolution was the presence of soldiers. The Continental Army and local militias were a common sight, their uniforms a reminder of the ongoing conflict. Betsy often saw young men, some barely older than boys, marching through the streets or gathered in the city squares. Their faces were a mix of resolve and weariness, a reflection of the hardships they endured. Betsy, like many others, did her best to support the soldiers, providing repairs to their uniforms or offering a kind word of encouragement.

The war also brought shortages and hardships. Basic supplies like food, clothing, and firewood became scarce. Prices soared, and the city experienced periods of intense scarcity. Betsy, with her resourcefulness and frugality learned from her Quaker upbringing, managed to make do with what she had. She grew vegetables in a small garden, preserved food for the winter, and found creative ways to stretch her resources. These skills were crucial not only for her survival but also for maintaining her business.

Philadelphia was not just a center of commerce

and military activity; it was also a place of ideas and debate. The city's coffeehouses and taverns buzzed with discussions about liberty, democracy, and the future of the colonies. Betsy occasionally found herself in these lively debates, her keen mind and strong opinions making her a valued participant. She listened to the impassioned speeches of patriots and shared her own thoughts on the need for independence and justice. These conversations were a reminder that the fight for freedom was not just on the battlefield but also in the hearts and minds of the people.

Despite the challenges, there were moments of joy and celebration. Betsy treasured the times when friends and family gathered, whether for a simple meal or a more festive occasion. These gatherings were filled with laughter, music, and stories, a respite from the harsh realities of war. Betsy's home became a sanctuary, a place where people could find warmth and companionship. Her ability to create a sense of home and comfort was a testament to her strength and resilience.

The arrival of important news was always a significant event. The sound of a rider galloping through the streets, bearing messages from the front lines or from Congress, would send a ripple of excitement through the city. Betsy, like everyone else, eagerly awaited updates on the progress of the war. Victories were celebrated with fervor, while defeats were met with renewed determination. The news brought a sense of connection to the broader struggle, reminding everyone that they were part of something much larger than themselves.

Amidst the daily routines and the constant backdrop of war, there were moments of profound change. The signing of the Declaration of Independence on July 4, 1776, was one such moment. Philadelphia was at the heart of this historic event, and the city erupted in celebration. Betsy, like many others, felt a deep sense of pride and hope. The declaration was a bold statement of the colonies' resolve and a promise of a new beginning. It was a reminder that their sacrifices and struggles were paving the way for a future of freedom and equality.

Betsy's life in Philadelphia during the American Revolution was a blend of the ordinary and the extraordinary. She balanced the demands of her business with the challenges of living in a war-torn city. Her days were filled with the hum of sewing, the chatter of the market, and the ever-present news of the conflict. Yet, through it all, she remained steadfast, her spirit unbroken by the hardships she faced.

the revolutionary war begins

The dawn of the Revolutionary War brought a wave of change that swept across the American colonies, and Philadelphia was at the epicenter of this upheaval. For Betsy Ross, the war's outbreak marked a period of profound personal and professional challenges, as well as moments of courage and resilience.

When the first shots were fired at Lexington and Concord in April 1775, the news quickly spread to Philadelphia, stirring a mix of fear, excitement, and determination among its residents. Betsy, now a widow running her upholstery business, felt the immediate impact of the war. The city buzzed with the energy of preparation and mobilization, and Betsy knew that life as she knew it would never be the same.

Betsy's family, like many others, was deeply affected by the war. Her father, Samuel Griscom, was a respected Quaker and a skilled carpenter. Though Quakers generally upheld pacifist beliefs, the war forced many, including Samuel, to confront difficult decisions about their involvement. The Griscom family held strong to their values, advocating for peace while also supporting the cause of independence in other ways.

One of the earliest and most significant impacts on Betsy's life was the increased demand for her upholstery services. The war effort required supplies and equipment, and Betsy's skills were in high demand for repairing uniforms, making tents, and crafting other essential items. Her workshop became a hive of activity, with orders coming in from local militias and Continental Army units. Betsy worked tirelessly, often late into the night, stitching and mending, knowing that her work was contributing to the larger struggle for freedom.

Despite the steady flow of work, the war brought economic instability. Prices for basic goods soared, and shortages became commonplace. Betsy, with her resourcefulness, managed to navigate these challenges. She bartered her services when necessary, trading her upholstery work for food, firewood, and other essentials. This adaptability was crucial for her survival and that of her business.

The war also brought personal loss and heartache. Betsy's brothers and other male relatives joined the fight for independence, leaving their families behind to worry about their safety. Letters from the front lines were rare and often filled with both hope and despair. Betsy anxiously awaited news of her loved ones, praying for their safe return. The uncertainty and fear weighed heavily on her, but she remained steadfast, finding strength in her work and her community.

Philadelphia itself was a city transformed by the war. It served as a hub for the Continental Congress, where pivotal decisions about the war and the future of the colonies were made. Betsy, living in such close proximity to these events, felt the intensity of the moment. The city was filled with soldiers, politicians, and patriots, all contributing to the cause in their own ways. The streets were often lined with troops marching to their next destination, and the air was thick with the tension of impending battles.

Amidst the turmoil, Betsy found moments of solace and solidarity. The community of Philadelphia was tight-knit, with neighbors supporting each other through the hardships. Betsy's home became a gathering place for friends and family, where they shared meals, stories, and encouragement. These gatherings were a respite from the harsh realities of war, providing a sense of normalcy and connection.

One particular evening, Betsy hosted a small group of friends and family. The mood was somber as they discussed the latest news from the front lines. One of Betsy's brothers, who had recently returned on leave, recounted his experiences in battle. His tales were filled with bravery and sacrifice, but also the grim realities of war. The group listened intently, their faces a mix of pride and concern. Betsy, ever the supportive sister, offered words of comfort and hope, reminding everyone of the importance of their struggle.

As the war progressed, the challenges grew more intense. The British occupation of Philadelphia in 1777 was a particularly difficult period. The city, once a bustling center of patriot activity, was now under enemy control. The British presence brought strict regulations and a sense of oppression. Betsy's business suffered during this time, as many of her clients were either fighting in the war or had fled the city. Supplies became even scarcer, and the threat of violence loomed over daily life.

Despite these hardships, Betsy remained resilient. She continued her work, often in secret, supporting the patriot cause in any way she could. Her home became a safe haven for those in need, offering shelter and aid to soldiers and civilians alike. Betsy's bravery and resourcefulness during the occupation earned her the respect and admiration of her peers.

The war also brought moments of unexpected

joy and inspiration. One such moment was the creation of the first American flag. Legend has it that in June 1776, Betsy was visited by George Washington, Robert Morris, and George Ross, who asked her to create a flag for the new nation. This request was a tremendous honor, and Betsy approached the task with both pride and meticulous care. She designed and stitched the flag, making it a symbol of hope and unity for the fledgling country.

The completion of the flag was a significant morale boost for Betsy and her community. It represented the ideals of freedom and independence that they were fighting for, and it became a rallying point for the patriot cause. Betsy's role in creating the flag cemented her place in American history, and it provided her with a sense of purpose and contribution amidst the chaos of war.

the birth of the american flag

meeting with george washington

IT WAS a warm afternoon in May 1776 when Betsy received an unexpected visit at her modest upholstery shop in Philadelphia. Betsy, ever industrious, was busy at her workbench, her hands deftly sewing a new set of drapes for a local family. The rhythmic sound of her needle moving through the fabric was soothing, a small comfort amidst the constant news of war and turmoil.

The door to her shop creaked open, and Betsy looked up to see three men entering. She recognized them immediately: George Washington, the esteemed commander-in-chief of the Continental Army; Robert Morris, a prominent financier and member of the Continental Congress; and George

Ross, her late husband's uncle and a respected patriot. The presence of these distinguished figures in her humble shop was both surprising and momentous.

Betsy wiped her hands on her apron and rose to greet them. "Good afternoon, gentlemen. How may I assist you today?" she asked, her voice calm and composed despite the flutter of nerves in her stomach.

Washington stepped forward, his tall frame and commanding presence filling the room. "Good afternoon, Mrs. Ross. We have come to request your expertise for a matter of great importance to our nation," he said, his tone respectful and earnest.

Betsy's curiosity was piqued. "Please, tell me more," she said, motioning for them to sit. The men took their seats, and Betsy joined them, eager to hear what had brought these notable leaders to her doorstep.

Robert Morris unrolled a parchment on the table, revealing a sketch of a flag. "As you know, our fight for independence is well underway. The Continental Congress has decided that our new nation needs a flag that will represent our unity and resolve. We have designed this flag, but we need someone with your skill to bring it to life," he explained.

Betsy examined the sketch closely. It featured thirteen alternating red and white stripes and thirteen six-pointed stars arranged in a circle on a field of blue. The design was striking, but she immediately noticed an area for improvement. "This is a fine design," she began, "but I believe the stars should have five points instead of six. It would be easier to cut and sew, and it would look just as beautiful."

The men exchanged glances, considering her suggestion. George Ross spoke up, "Can you demonstrate what you mean, Betsy?"

Betsy nodded and reached for a piece of paper. She folded it carefully and, with a single snip of her scissors, produced a perfect five-pointed star. She handed it to Washington, who examined it with keen interest. "This is indeed simpler and quite elegant," he said, a hint of admiration in his voice.

Washington's approval settled the matter. "Very well, Mrs. Ross. We trust your judgment and skill. Please, make the necessary adjustments and create the first flag of our new nation."

Betsy felt a surge of pride and responsibility. "I will do my best, General Washington. You can count on me," she replied with determination.

With the meeting concluded, the men left Betsy's shop, leaving her with the task that would soon become an iconic symbol of American independence. Betsy wasted no time, gathering the materials she needed: red, white, and blue fabric, strong thread, and her trusty sewing tools. She set up her workbench with the precision and care that had become second nature to her.

As she began cutting the fabric into stripes and stars, Betsy's mind was filled with thoughts of the brave soldiers fighting for freedom, including her own family members. She worked methodically, each stitch a testament to her commitment and her hope for a brighter future. The hours passed quickly, and Betsy's hands moved with practiced ease, transforming the raw materials into a beautiful flag.

Late into the night, with the candles burning low, Betsy paused to admire her progress. The flag was nearly complete, its colors vibrant and its design bold. She felt a deep sense of satisfaction, knowing that this flag would soon fly over the troops, inspiring them in their fight for independence.

The next morning, Betsy added the finishing touches, ensuring that every seam was secure and every star perfectly positioned. She carefully folded the flag and placed it in a protective cloth, ready for its journey to the Continental Congress.

When the men returned to her shop to see the finished flag, their reactions were immediate and heartfelt. George Washington held the flag up to the light, his eyes reflecting the significance of the moment. "Mrs. Ross, this is magnificent. You have done a great service to your country," he said, his voice filled with genuine admiration.

Robert Morris and George Ross echoed his sentiments, expressing their gratitude and appreciation for Betsy's exceptional work. The flag was presented to the Continental Congress, and it was quickly adopted as the official emblem of the United States. Betsy's creation became a powerful symbol of unity, courage, and the unwavering spirit of the American people.

The story of Betsy Ross and her meeting with George Washington became a cherished part of American folklore, a tale of quiet heroism and the impact of individual contributions. While historians continue to debate the specifics of the legend, the essence of the story remains a testament to the enduring values of ingenuity, patriotism, and resilience.

Betsy Ross's role in creating the first American flag was more than a historical footnote; it was a reflection of her character and her unwavering commitment to the cause of independence. Her meeting with George Washington and the subsequent creation of the flag showcased her ability to rise to the occasion, to use her skills for a greater purpose, and to leave an indelible mark on the fabric of American history.

designing the flag

Betsy began by gathering the necessary materials. She selected high-quality wool bunting in red, white, and blue—the traditional colors that would come to symbolize valor, purity, and perseverance. She laid out the fabrics in her modest workshop, the bright colors a stark contrast to the simple wooden furniture and plain walls. Each color carried its own significance and weight, reflecting the values and aspirations of the emerging nation.

Her first task was to cut the thirteen stripes that would form the foundation of the flag. Each stripe needed to be precisely measured and carefully cut to ensure they were even and proportional. Betsy's hands moved with practiced ease, her scissors gliding through the fabric with precision. The red and white stripes were arranged in an alternating pattern, symbolizing the original thirteen colonies that had come together in the fight for independence.

Next, Betsy turned her attention to the field of blue, where the stars would be placed. She meticulously measured and cut a large blue square, making sure it was perfectly symmetrical. The stars themselves were a crucial element of the design. Betsy's suggestion to use five-pointed stars had been accepted, and she was determined to create each one with care and accuracy.

Betsy's method for creating the stars was both ingenious and efficient. She folded small pieces of white fabric into a specific pattern, then made a single cut with her scissors. When she unfolded the fabric, a perfect five-pointed star emerged. This technique allowed her to produce uniform stars quickly, ensuring consistency across the flag. She repeated this process thirteen times, each star representing one of the colonies that had united in the struggle for freedom.

With the stars ready, Betsy carefully arranged them on the blue field. She decided to place them in a circular pattern, symbolizing unity and equality among the colonies. The circle had no beginning and no end, representing the enduring and inclusive nature of the new nation. Betsy pinned the stars in place, stepping back to admire the layout before sewing them down. The sight of the stars, bright and hopeful against the deep blue fabric, filled her with a sense of purpose and pride.

Sewing the stars onto the blue field required patience and precision. Betsy used small, tight stitches to secure each star, ensuring they would withstand the wear and tear of time and weather. As she worked, she thought about the soldiers who would fight under this flag, the people who would look to it for inspiration, and the future generations who would inherit the values it represented.

Once the stars were securely in place, Betsy began the process of assembling the flag. She sewed the blue field onto the top left corner of the striped fabric, aligning it carefully to ensure a seamless integration. Her needle moved swiftly but deliberately, each stitch reinforcing the bond between the stripes and the stars. The flag was coming together beautifully, a testament to Betsy's skill and dedication.

As she worked, Betsy often reflected on the significance of the flag and her role in its creation. She knew that this symbol would carry the hopes and dreams of a nation striving for independence. It was more than just a piece of fabric; it was a statement of identity, a beacon of unity, and a call to arms. Betsy felt a deep connection to this project, recognizing that her contribution was part of a larger, collective effort to build a new nation.

The final step in the creation of the flag was to hem the edges, ensuring that it would not fray or unravel. Betsy took great care in this task, knowing that the durability of the flag was just as important as its design. Her hands moved with steady confidence, her stitches precise and even. She reinforced the corners, adding extra strength to withstand the winds that would whip across battlefields and city squares.

When the flag was finally complete, Betsy laid it out before her, the colors vibrant and the design striking. She felt a profound sense of accomplishment, knowing that she had played a part in shaping the symbol of a new nation. The flag was more than just her handiwork; it was a reflection of the values and aspirations that had driven the colonies to seek independence.

The following day, Betsy carefully folded the flag and placed it in a protective cloth, ready for its journey to the Continental Congress. She felt a mix of excitement and nervousness as she prepared to present her work to the men who had entrusted her with this important task. She knew that the flag would soon be seen by many, its presence a powerful reminder of the unity and resolve of the American people.

When George Washington, Robert Morris, and George Ross returned to her shop to see the finished flag, their reactions were immediate and heartfelt. They were deeply moved by the craftsmanship and beauty of Betsy's work, recognizing that she had not only met their expectations but exceeded them. Washington held the flag up to the light, his eyes reflecting the significance of the moment. "Mrs. Ross, this is magnificent. You have done a great service to your country," he said, his voice filled with genuine admiration.

Robert Morris and George Ross echoed his sentiments, expressing their gratitude and appreciation for Betsy's exceptional work. The flag was presented to the Continental Congress, where it was adopted as the official emblem of the United States. Betsy's creation became a powerful symbol of unity, courage, and the unwavering spirit of the American people.

6 /
betsy's challenges

perseverance

EACH MORNING, Betsy began her day before dawn, her routine a comforting anchor in the midst of chaos. The first light of the day found her preparing a simple breakfast, the quiet of the early hours offering a brief respite from the noise of war. Her thoughts often turned to John, but instead of letting her grief overwhelm her, Betsy channeled her emotions into her work. She knew that maintaining her upholstery business was not only vital for her survival but also her way of contributing to the cause of independence.

The city of Philadelphia was a hive of activity, its streets filled with soldiers, merchants, and fellow citizens trying to carry on with their lives amidst the turmoil. Betsy's workshop, a small yet vibrant space, was a microcosm of this larger world. Rolls of fabric, spools of thread, and various tools filled the room, a testament to her relentless effort to keep her business running. Each piece of furniture she upholstered, each garment she mended, was done with precision and care, a silent act of defiance against the disorder outside.

One of Betsy's most significant challenges was the scarcity of supplies. The war had disrupted trade routes, making it difficult to obtain the materials she needed. Betsy's resourcefulness came to the fore as she navigated these shortages. She learned to make do with less, repurposing old fabrics and finding innovative ways to stretch her resources. Her ability to adapt and improvise became a crucial part of her daily routine.

The financial strain was another constant concern. With John gone, Betsy had to single-handedly manage the business's finances. She meticulously recorded every transaction, ensuring that not a penny was wasted. Her clients, many of whom were struggling themselves, appreciated her fairness and reliability. Betsy's reputation for honesty and quality work spread, bringing in a steady, albeit modest, stream of business.

One day, a local militia captain visited Betsy's

workshop with a special request. His regiment needed new uniforms, but funds and materials were limited. Betsy agreed to take on the project, understanding the critical role these soldiers played in the fight for independence. She spent long hours sewing the uniforms, her hands moving swiftly and surely. Each stitch was a labor of love, a small yet meaningful contribution to the war effort. When the captain returned to collect the finished uniforms, he expressed his deep gratitude, knowing that Betsy's hard work would help keep his men clothed and warm.

The British occupation of Philadelphia in 1777 brought additional challenges. The city, once a stronghold of patriot activity, was now under enemy control. The atmosphere was tense, with curfews and restrictions imposed on the residents. Betsy's business suffered during this time, as many of her clients had fled the city or were unable to pay for her services. Despite these setbacks, Betsy remained resilient. She found ways to continue her work in secret, supporting the patriot cause in any way she could.

One evening, as she was working late into the night, Betsy heard a soft knock at her door. She opened it to find a young soldier, exhausted and in need of help. His uniform was torn, and he carried a letter from a mutual acquaintance asking for Betsy's assistance. Without hesitation, Betsy welcomed him in, offering food and a place to rest. She repaired his uniform, stitching the fabric with care and precision. The soldier's gratitude was palpable, and Betsy felt a renewed sense of purpose. Her small acts of kindness and defiance were her way of fighting back, of contributing to the greater cause.

Betsy's perseverance extended beyond her professional life. She remained deeply involved in her community, offering support to friends and neighbors who were also struggling. Her home became a sanctuary for those in need, a place where people could find comfort and assistance. Betsy's ability to provide emotional and practical support to others was a testament to her strength and compassion.

Her family was a crucial source of support during these difficult times. Betsy's parents, siblings, and extended family rallied around her, offering help whenever they could. This close-knit network provided a safety net, allowing Betsy to focus on her work and her contributions to the war effort. Family gatherings, though less frequent due to the war, were moments of solace and connection.

They shared stories, offered encouragement, and found strength in their shared experiences.

Amidst the hardships, there were moments of triumph that fueled Betsy's determination. The flag she had created became a powerful symbol of hope and resilience, not just for the nation but for Betsy herself. The sight of the flag flying proudly in the streets of Philadelphia, over battlefields, and in encampments was a reminder of the values she held dear. It represented unity, courage, and the relentless pursuit of freedom—values that guided her every action.

One particularly memorable moment came when Betsy received a letter from one of her brothers who was fighting in the Continental Army. He described how the sight of the flag had lifted the spirits of the soldiers, giving them the strength to continue their fight. His words filled Betsy with pride and renewed resolve. She knew that her work, though often done in the quiet of her workshop, was making a significant impact.

betsy's later years

continued contributions

THE POST-WAR PERIOD brought a mix of relief and new challenges. The city of Philadelphia was bustling with activity, as soldiers returned home and the economy began to recover. Betsy, who had maintained her upholstery business throughout the war, found herself in high demand. People needed their homes repaired and refurnished, and Betsy's reputation for quality work and reliability ensured a steady stream of clients.

One of Betsy's first major projects after the war was restoring a set of fine furniture for a prominent Philadelphia family. The pieces had been damaged during the British occupation, and the family sought Betsy's expertise to bring them back to their former glory. This project was particularly rewarding for Betsy, as it symbolized the city's recovery and the return to normalcy. She carefully selected materials and employed her best techniques, transforming the worn and damaged furniture into stunning pieces that reflected her craftsmanship and dedication.

Beyond her business, Betsy remained deeply involved in her community. The war had left many families struggling, and Betsy was always ready to lend a hand. She organized efforts to provide food and clothing to those in need, using her skills to mend and create garments for children and adults alike. Her home continued to be a place of refuge and support, where friends and neighbors could find comfort and assistance.

Betsy's patriotism and commitment to the new nation were unwavering. She often spoke about the importance of unity and the need to support the country's leaders as they worked to build a stable and prosperous government. Her experience during the war had shown her the strength and resilience of the American people, and she believed deeply in the nation's potential.

As the United States began to establish its identity, there was a growing demand for symbols that represented the nation's ideals. Betsy found herself once again at the forefront of this effort. She received numerous requests to create flags and other emblems that would be used in public buildings, schools, and military installations. Each project was an opportunity for Betsy to contribute to the nation's evolving identity, and she approached each one with the same care and dedication that had characterized her earlier work.

One particularly significant project was creating a large flag for the Pennsylvania State House, now known as Independence Hall. This building held great historical importance, as it was where the Declaration of Independence had been signed. Betsy felt a deep sense of pride and responsibility as she worked on this flag, knowing that it would hang in a place that symbolized the birth of the nation. The flag was a masterpiece of her craft, with vibrant colors and precise stitching that reflected her unwavering commitment to excellence.

Betsy's work extended beyond flags and upholstery. She became an advocate for the preservation of historical artifacts and documents, understanding the importance of maintaining a tangible connection to the past. She worked with local historians and civic leaders to ensure that important items from the Revolutionary War were preserved and displayed for future generations. Betsy's efforts helped to establish some of the first historical societies in the country, laying the groundwork for the preservation of American heritage.

As a respected member of the community, Betsy also played a role in educating the next generation. She often welcomed young apprentices into her workshop, teaching them the skills of sewing and upholstery. These sessions were more than just lessons in craftsmanship; they were opportunities for Betsy to impart values of hard work, dedication, and patriotism. She enjoyed watching her apprentices grow and develop their own talents, knowing that she was contributing to their futures and to the future of the nation.

Betsy's personal life also saw new developments. In 1783, she married Joseph Ashburn, a sea captain who had been a prisoner of war during the conflict. Their marriage brought Betsy happiness and companionship, though it was again marked by tragedy when Joseph was captured by the British and died in a prison in England. Despite this loss, Betsy's resilience shone through. She continued her work, driven by a sense of purpose and a commitment to the ideals of the new nation.

Later, Betsy married John Claypoole, a fellow patriot and friend from her past. Their marriage was a source of joy and stability for Betsy. John shared her values and supported her work, and together they created a loving home. The couple raised Betsy's daughters and lived a life marked by mutual respect and shared dedication to their community.

Betsy's contributions during this period were not limited to her professional and civic activities. She was also deeply involved in the social and political life of Philadelphia. She participated in various civic organizations and was a regular presence at public meetings and events. Her insights and opinions were valued by her peers, and she became a trusted voice in discussions about the future of the city and the nation.

One notable aspect of Betsy's continued contributions was her involvement in charitable work. She helped to establish and support several charitable organizations that provided assistance to widows, orphans, and veterans. Betsy's own experiences had made her acutely aware of the challenges faced by those who had lost loved ones or were struggling to make ends meet. Her compassion and generosity made a significant difference in the lives of many people in her community.

family life

Following the death of her first husband, John Ross, Betsy faced the challenges of widowhood with strength and determination. Her life took a new turn in 1783 when she met Joseph Ashburn, a sea captain who had served in the war. Joseph was kind and attentive, offering Betsy the companionship and support she deeply needed. They married, and Betsy embraced the new chapter in her life with hope.

Life with Joseph brought both happiness and hardship. The nature of his work as a sea captain meant that Joseph was often away, leaving Betsy to manage their home and business. Despite these absences, their time together was filled with love and mutual respect. Betsy admired Joseph's courage and dedication, and they shared dreams of a peaceful and prosperous future.

Their happiness was short-lived, however. During one of his voyages, Joseph was captured by the British and imprisoned in England. Betsy was devastated by the news but held onto hope for his return. She continued her work, using it as a source of strength and distraction from the uncertainty surrounding Joseph's fate.

The news of Joseph's death in a British prison

was a crushing blow. Betsy was once again thrust into the depths of grief, but her resilience shone through. She had her daughters to care for and a business to run, and she knew she needed to remain strong for their sake. Her community rallied around her, offering support and comfort during this difficult time.

Amidst this period of loss, Betsy found solace in her work and the love of her children. She was a devoted mother, balancing her responsibilities as a businesswoman with the demands of raising her daughters. Her home was filled with laughter and learning, as she taught her children the values of hard work, kindness, and perseverance. Betsy's daughters grew up in an environment rich with love and support, learning from their mother's example of resilience and dedication.

Betsy's life took another positive turn when she reconnected with John Claypoole, a fellow patriot and old friend. John had also endured significant hardships during the war, including being a prisoner of war. Their shared experiences and mutual respect drew them together, and they married in 1783. This marriage brought Betsy much-needed stability and happiness.

John was a supportive and loving husband who admired Betsy's strength and character. Their home became a place of warmth and joy, where they raised Betsy's daughters together. John's presence brought a sense of security and partnership that Betsy had longed for. He supported her in her business endeavors and encouraged her involvement in the community.

The Claypoole household was a lively and bustling place. Betsy's daughters thrived under the care and guidance of both their mother and John. Family life was filled with shared meals, lively discussions, and the simple pleasures of daily routines. Betsy and John worked side by side in the upholstery business, their collaboration strengthening both their relationship and their livelihood.

Betsy's commitment to her family extended beyond her immediate household. She remained close to her parents, siblings, and extended family, ensuring that her children were connected to their larger family network. Family gatherings were a source of joy and a reminder of the enduring bonds that supported them through difficult times.

The values Betsy instilled in her children were a reflection of her own principles. She emphasized the importance of hard work, honesty, and compassion. Her daughters watched her navigate the challenges of life with grace and determination, learning valuable lessons that would guide them in their own lives. Betsy's example of resilience and dedication left a lasting impact on her children, shaping them into strong and capable individuals.

Betsy's role as a mother was complemented by her continued involvement in her community. She was a respected figure in Philadelphia, known for her charitable work and civic engagement. Betsy's home often served as a gathering place for discussions on important issues, and she was actively involved in efforts to support widows, orphans, and veterans. Her compassion and generosity extended beyond her family, making a significant difference in the lives of many in her community.

Betsy's life with John Claypoole was marked by a sense of fulfillment and peace. Together, they navigated the challenges of post-war America, contributing to the rebuilding and growth of their community. Their partnership was a testament to the power of love and mutual respect, providing a strong foundation for their family.

As Betsy's children grew older, they began to forge their own paths, but the values and lessons they had learned from their mother remained with them. Betsy's influence was evident in their choices and actions, a legacy of strength and integrity that she had imparted through her own life.

betsy ross's legacy

historical impact

THE FLAG'S journey from Betsy's small workshop to becoming an emblem of a nation was a testament to its profound significance. When the Continental Congress adopted the flag in 1777, it marked a formal recognition of the colonies' unity and shared purpose. The flag, with its thirteen red and white stripes and thirteen stars arranged in a circle, symbolized the original colonies' commitment to stand together against British tyranny.

As the flag began to fly over military encampments, government buildings, and public gatherings, it quickly became a source of inspiration and pride. For the soldiers on the front lines, the sight of the flag waving in the breeze was a powerful reminder of what they were fighting for. It represented the ideals of liberty and justice, and it gave them the strength to persevere even in the face of overwhelming odds.

One of the most iconic moments in the flag's early history was its presence at the Battle of Fort Stanwix in 1777. The fort, located in what is now Rome, New York, was under siege by British forces. The American defenders, lacking a formal flag, created one using a combination of materials at hand, including a red petticoat. When the newly adopted flag arrived, it replaced the makeshift version, boosting the morale of the troops. The flag's appearance at Fort Stanwix became a symbol of resilience and determination, underscoring the importance of unity in the fight for independence.

The flag also played a significant role in the diplomatic efforts of the young nation. When American envoys traveled to foreign courts seeking support and recognition, they carried the flag as a symbol of the new nation's sovereignty and ideals. The flag was a visual representation of the United States' commitment to the principles of democracy and self-determination. It helped to forge alliances and secure aid from foreign powers, contributing to the eventual victory in the Revolutionary War.

In the years following the war, the flag

continued to serve as a unifying symbol for the fledgling nation. As the United States expanded westward and new states were added to the Union, the flag evolved to reflect the changing composition of the country. The original thirteen stars grew to fifteen, then twenty, and eventually to fifty, each new star representing a new state joining the Union. Despite these changes, the core design of the flag remained constant, a testament to its enduring significance.

Betsy Ross's role in creating the first flag became a cherished part of American folklore. Her story was passed down through generations, celebrated in history books, and commemorated in public ceremonies. The legend of Betsy Ross and the first flag became an integral part of the national narrative, symbolizing the contributions of ordinary citizens to the cause of independence. Her story highlighted the role of women in the Revolution, acknowledging their efforts and sacrifices in support of the fight for freedom.

The historical impact of Betsy Ross's flag extended beyond the Revolutionary War. During the Civil War, the flag became a powerful symbol of unity and perseverance. As the nation faced its greatest internal conflict, the flag served as a reminder of the ideals that had brought the country together. It was a symbol of the fight to preserve the Union and the struggle to extend the principles of liberty and justice to all Americans.

In the modern era, the flag has continued to play a central role in American identity. It is a symbol of national pride, flown at government buildings, schools, and homes across the country. The flag is present at significant moments in American history, from inaugurations and public celebrations to moments of mourning and remembrance. It is a constant reminder of the values that underpin the nation and the sacrifices made to uphold them.

One of the most poignant displays of the flag's significance occurred in the aftermath of the September 11, 2001, terrorist attacks. The image of firefighters raising the flag amidst the rubble of the World Trade Center became an enduring symbol of resilience and hope. The flag, once again, served as a unifying force, bringing Americans together in the face of tragedy and reaffirming their commitment to the principles of freedom and democracy.

Betsy Ross's flag has also had a significant cultural impact. It has been featured in countless works of art, literature, and music, becoming an emblem of American creativity and expression. The flag's design, with its bold colors and simple geometry, has inspired artists and designers, symbolizing both the nation's history and its future. The flag is a common motif in American pop culture, appearing in everything from fashion to film, reinforcing its status as a powerful national symbol.

The educational value of the flag's history is also profound. Schoolchildren across the United States learn about Betsy Ross and the creation of the first flag as part of their studies on the American Revolution. The story of the flag serves as an entry point for discussions about the founding principles of the nation, the struggles and sacrifices of the Revolutionary War, and the role of individuals in shaping history. Betsy Ross's legacy is a powerful reminder that history is made not only by famous leaders but also by the contributions of ordinary people.

remembering betsy

One of the most prominent tributes to Betsy Ross is the Betsy Ross House in Philadelphia, where she is believed to have lived and sewn the first American flag. The house, a modest yet charming structure, has been meticulously preserved as a historic site. Visitors from around the world come to the Betsy Ross House to step back in time and experience a piece of American history.

The Betsy Ross House is located in the heart of Philadelphia's historic district, surrounded by other significant landmarks such as Independence Hall and the Liberty Bell. As visitors approach the house, they are greeted by a cobblestone courtyard and the sight of the American flag proudly flying above. The exterior of the house, with its classic colonial architecture, provides a glimpse into the 18th-century life that Betsy Ross would have known.

Inside the Betsy Ross House, each room is carefully curated to reflect the period in which Betsy lived and worked. The first floor features a cozy parlor and a functional workshop, where Betsy would have spent countless hours sewing and crafting. Authentic period furnishings, tools, and decorations create an immersive experience, allowing visitors to feel as though they have stepped into Betsy's world.

One of the highlights of the house is the upstairs bedroom, where a replica of Betsy's original flag is displayed. This room often evokes a sense of awe and reverence, as visitors reflect on the significance of the flag and the woman who created it. Guided tours provide detailed insights into Betsy's life, her contributions, and the broader context of the American Revolution. Knowledgeable guides share stories and anecdotes, bringing Betsy's legacy to life in a way that is both educational and engaging.

The Betsy Ross House also hosts a variety of educational programs and events aimed at both children and adults. School groups frequently visit the house as part of their history curriculum, learning about the American Revolution and the role of women in the fight for independence. Interactive workshops allow students to try their hand at sewing, using techniques similar to those Betsy would have employed. These hands-on experiences help to deepen their understanding and appreciation of history.

In addition to school programs, the Betsy Ross House offers special events throughout the year. Flag Day celebrations, held annually on June 14th, are particularly popular. The festivities include flag-raising ceremonies, historical reenactments, and educational activities that honor Betsy's contributions and the significance of the American flag. These events draw large crowds and foster a sense of community and national pride.

Betsy Ross is also commemorated through various monuments and memorials across the United States. In Philadelphia, a statue of Betsy Ross stands proudly in a public park, capturing her spirit and determination. The statue, often adorned with flowers and flags, serves as a reminder of her enduring legacy. Similar memorials can be found in other cities, each one a tribute to the impact Betsy had on American history.

Educational institutions and organizations also play a key role in preserving and promoting Betsy Ross's legacy. Many schools and libraries include her story in their history lessons, ensuring that students understand the importance of her contributions. Books, documentaries, and online resources provide further opportunities for people to learn about Betsy's life and the creation of the first American flag. These educational efforts help to keep her memory alive and relevant in contemporary society.

The story of Betsy Ross and the American flag is also a common theme in cultural and artistic expressions. Paintings, songs, and plays have been created to celebrate her legacy and the symbol she helped to create. These works of art capture the imagination and convey the emotional and historical significance of Betsy's contribution. They serve as a testament to the enduring power of her story and its ability to inspire creativity and patriotism.

In popular culture, Betsy Ross remains a recognizable and respected figure. Her name is often invoked in discussions about American history and the founding of the nation. She is featured in museums and exhibitions, where her story is presented alongside those of other key figures from the Revolutionary era. Her life and work continue to be a source of fascination and admiration, highlighting the vital role of individuals in shaping history.

Betsy Ross's legacy is also reflected in the continued use and evolution of the American flag. As a symbol, the flag represents the values and principles that Betsy and her contemporaries fought for. It is a constant presence in American life, flown at public buildings, homes, and events. The flag's design, rooted in Betsy's original creation, has become an enduring emblem of the nation's identity and aspirations.

conclusion

Betsy Ross lived in a time of great upheaval and change. The American Revolution was a period of uncertainty and conflict, demanding immense bravery and determination from everyone involved. Betsy, despite facing personal losses and societal challenges, remained steadfast in her resolve. Her ability to persevere through adversity and contribute to the war effort highlighted her inner strength and resilience.

One of the most remarkable aspects of Betsy's story is her willingness to step forward when her skills were needed. When George Washington and other leaders sought someone to create a flag for the new nation, Betsy didn't hesitate. She took on the challenge with confidence, knowing that her work would represent the ideals and aspirations of an entire country. This decision required not only technical skill but also immense courage. Betsy understood the significance of her task and rose to the occasion, transforming a simple request into a lasting symbol of independence.

Creativity played a central role in Betsy's life and contributions. Her suggestion to change the flag's stars from six points to five was a brilliant example of practical ingenuity. This change made the flag easier to produce and more aesthetically pleasing, showcasing Betsy's ability to think critically and innovate. Her creative approach extended beyond the flag, influencing her upholstery work and her problem-solving in daily life. Betsy's creativity was a driving force behind her success, allowing her to navigate challenges with grace and resourcefulness.

Betsy's story also emphasizes the importance of using one's talents for the greater good. Her skills as a seamstress and upholsterer were instrumental in supporting the American cause. She didn't just view her work as a means of personal livelihood but as a way to contribute to something larger than herself. This sense of purpose and dedication to community is a powerful lesson for readers of all ages. Betsy's example encourages us to look for ways to use our abilities to make a positive impact on the world around us.

The courage and creativity that Betsy demonstrated are qualities that remain relevant today. In our modern world, we face our own set of challenges and uncertainties. Betsy's story reminds us that we all have the capacity to rise above our circumstances and make a difference. Whether it's through innovation, perseverance, or a commitment to our values, we can all find ways to contribute meaningfully to our communities and society.

Betsy's legacy is a reminder that age and background do not limit one's ability to make a significant impact. Betsy was a young woman in a male-dominated society, yet she made her mark on history through her courage and creativity. Her story inspires children to believe in their potential and to pursue their passions with confidence. It teaches them that their ideas and actions can shape the world in profound ways.

For career professionals, Betsy's life offers valuable insights into the power of resilience and innovation. Her ability to adapt to changing circumstances, her commitment to excellence, and her creative problem-solving are qualities that are highly relevant in any professional setting. Betsy's story encourages professionals to approach their work with a sense of purpose and to look for innovative solutions to the challenges they face. It reminds them that courage and creativity are key drivers of success and impact.

Betsy's legacy is also a celebration of the American spirit. The flag she created has become a symbol of the values that define the United States: liberty, justice, and unity. Her story is a reminder of the importance of these values and the role that each individual can play in upholding them. Betsy's life teaches us that courage and creativity are not just personal virtues but essential components of a thriving and just society.

As we reflect on Betsy Ross's legacy, it is important to remember that her story is not just a historical anecdote but a living inspiration. Her courage and creativity continue to resonate, encouraging us to face our challenges with resilience and to approach our opportunities with innovation. Betsy's example reminds us that history is shaped by individuals who dare to dream and to act on their convictions.

Visiting the Betsy Ross House, learning about her contributions, and seeing the flag she created are all ways to connect with her legacy. These experiences bring her story to life, allowing us to appreciate the depth of her impact and the relevance of her values. Betsy's life serves as a bridge between the past and the present, linking the struggles and triumphs of the American Revolution with the ongoing journey of the nation.

activities

flag-making activity

Creating your own flag can be a fun and meaningful way to connect with the story of Betsy Ross and the creation of the first American flag. This hands-on activity will help you understand the craftsmanship and creativity that went into making the original flag while also allowing you to express your own artistic flair. Let's get started on making a simple yet beautiful flag!

Materials You'll Need:

- A piece of white fabric (about 12 x 18 inches)

- Red and blue fabric or felt (you can also use colored paper if fabric isn't available)

- Scissors

- Fabric glue or a hot glue gun

- Ruler

- Pencil

- Needle and thread (optional for more advanced crafters)

- A wooden dowel or a sturdy stick for the flagpole

- Markers or fabric paint (optional for decorating)

Step-by-Step Instructions:

1. Prepare the Base Fabric: Start with a piece of white fabric measuring about 12 x 18 inches. This will be the base of your flag. If you don't have fabric, a sturdy piece of white paper can work as well.

2. Cut the Stripes: Take your red fabric or felt and cut seven strips, each about 1 inch wide and 18 inches long. These stripes represent the original thirteen colonies and will be placed horizontally across the flag. If you're using paper, cut out the same number of red strips.

3. Arrange the Stripes: Lay out your white fabric base on a flat surface. Starting from the top, arrange

the red stripes evenly across the fabric, with the first stripe at the top edge. Alternate with the white spaces in between the red stripes, ensuring they are evenly spaced. You should have a total of 13 stripes (7 red and 6 white).

4. Attach the Stripes: Use fabric glue or a hot glue gun to secure the stripes onto the white fabric. If you prefer, you can sew the stripes on using a needle and thread, which will give your flag a more authentic feel.

5. Create the Blue Field: Cut a blue square measuring about 6 x 6 inches from your blue fabric or felt. This square will be placed in the top left corner of your flag, representing the union of the colonies.

6. Add the Stars: Using white fabric or felt, cut out five-pointed stars. You can create a stencil by folding a piece of paper and cutting a star shape, then using it to trace and cut your stars. For simplicity, let's start with five stars, but you can add more if you like.

7. Arrange and Attach the Stars: Place the blue square in the top left corner of your flag and

arrange the stars evenly on it. Use fabric glue or a hot glue gun to attach the stars to the blue field. If you're up for a challenge, you can sew the stars onto the blue fabric.

8. Attach the Blue Field to the Flag: Once your stars are securely in place, attach the blue square to the top left corner of your flag using fabric glue, a hot glue gun, or a needle and thread.

9. Secure the Flag to the Pole: Take your wooden dowel or sturdy stick and attach the left edge of your flag to it. You can use fabric glue, a hot glue gun, or stitch it on. Make sure the flag is securely fastened so it doesn't come loose when you wave it.

10. Optional Decoration: If you'd like to personalize your flag further, use markers or fabric paint to add additional designs or messages. This is a great way to express your creativity and make the flag uniquely yours.

11. Wave Your Flag Proudly: Your flag is now complete! Take a moment to admire your handiwork and think about the history and significance behind the flag you created. Just like Betsy Ross,

you've used your creativity and craftsmanship to make something meaningful.

quaker recipes

Cooking in the 18th century was a vital part of daily life, and the Quaker community had its own unique recipes that were simple, wholesome, and delicious. These recipes provide a delightful way to connect with history and enjoy a taste of the past. Let's explore some traditional Quaker recipes that kids can try, bringing a bit of the 18th century into your kitchen.

1. Johnnycakes

Johnnycakes, also known as journey cakes, are a type of cornmeal flatbread that were a staple in 18th-century kitchens. They are easy to make and can be enjoyed with butter, honey, or maple syrup.

Ingredients:
- 1 cup cornmeal
- 1 cup boiling water
- 1/2 teaspoon salt
- Butter or oil for frying

Instructions:

1. In a mixing bowl, combine the cornmeal and salt.

2. Pour the boiling water over the cornmeal mixture and stir until it forms a thick batter.

3. Let the batter sit for a few minutes to cool and thicken.

4. Heat a skillet over medium heat and add a small amount of butter or oil.

5. Drop spoonfuls of the batter onto the skillet, flattening them into small cakes with the back of the spoon.

6. Cook the johnnycakes for about 2-3 minutes on each side, until they are golden brown and crispy.

7. Serve warm with butter, honey, or maple syrup.

2. Gingerbread Cookies

Gingerbread cookies were a popular treat in the 18th century, enjoyed especially during festive occasions. These cookies are spiced with ginger and molasses, giving them a warm, rich flavor.

Ingredients:

- 2 1/2 cups flour

- 1/2 teaspoon baking soda

- 1/4 teaspoon salt

- 1 teaspoon ground ginger

- 1 teaspoon ground cinnamon

- 1/2 teaspoon ground cloves

- 1/2 cup butter, softened

- 1/2 cup brown sugar

- 1/2 cup molasses

- 1 egg

Instructions:

1. In a bowl, whisk together the flour, baking soda, salt, ginger, cinnamon, and cloves.

2. In a separate bowl, cream together the butter and brown sugar until light and fluffy.

3. Beat in the egg and molasses until well combined.

4. Gradually add the dry ingredients to the wet mixture, mixing until a dough forms.

5. Divide the dough in half, flatten each half into a disk, and wrap in plastic wrap. Refrigerate for at least 1 hour.

6. Preheat the oven to 350°F (175°C). Line baking sheets with parchment paper.

7. On a lightly floured surface, roll out the dough to about 1/4 inch thick. Use cookie cutters to cut out shapes.

8. Place the cookies on the prepared baking sheets and bake for 8-10 minutes, until the edges are lightly browned.

9. Let the cookies cool on the baking sheets for a few minutes, then transfer to a wire rack to cool completely.

10. Decorate with icing if desired, or enjoy them plain.

3. Apple Tansey

Apple tansey is a simple, sweet omelet made with apples and cinnamon. It was a common breakfast or dessert dish in the 18th century.

Ingredients:
- 2 apples, peeled, cored, and thinly sliced
- 2 tablespoons butter
- 4 eggs
- 1/4 cup milk
- 1 tablespoon sugar
- 1/2 teaspoon ground cinnamon
- 1/4 teaspoon ground nutmeg

Instructions:
1. In a large skillet, melt the butter over medium heat.

2. Add the apple slices and cook until they are soft and golden brown, about 5-7 minutes.

3. In a bowl, whisk together the eggs, milk, sugar, cinnamon, and nutmeg.

4. Pour the egg mixture over the apples in the skillet.

5. Cook without stirring until the eggs are set and the bottom is golden brown, about 5 minutes. You can lift the edges gently with a spatula to let uncooked egg run underneath if needed.

6. Carefully flip the omelet and cook for an additional 2-3 minutes until fully cooked.

7. Slide the apple tansey onto a plate, cut into wedges, and serve warm.

4. Hasty Pudding

Hasty pudding is a simple and hearty porridge made from cornmeal, a staple in colonial kitchens. It can be served as a sweet or savory dish.

Ingredients:

- 1 cup cornmeal

- 4 cups water

- 1/2 teaspoon salt

- Butter, honey, or maple syrup for serving (optional)

Instructions:

1. In a saucepan, bring 3 cups of water to a boil.

2. In a separate bowl, mix the cornmeal with the remaining 1 cup of water to make a smooth paste.

3. Gradually stir the cornmeal mixture into the boiling water, whisking constantly to prevent lumps.

4. Add the salt and reduce the heat to low.

5. Cook, stirring frequently, until the mixture thickens and the cornmeal is tender, about 15-20 minutes.

6. Serve warm, topped with butter, honey, or maple syrup if desired.

5. Quaker Oat Cakes

Quaker oat cakes are a simple and nutritious snack made from oats, a staple in Quaker diets. These cakes are easy to make and perfect for a healthy treat.

Ingredients:

- 2 cups rolled oats
- 1/4 cup brown sugar
- 1/4 cup melted butter
- 1/4 cup honey
- 1/4 teaspoon salt

- 1/2 teaspoon ground cinnamon

- 1/4 cup milk

Instructions:

1. Preheat the oven to 350°F (175°C). Line a baking sheet with parchment paper.

2. In a large bowl, combine the rolled oats, brown sugar, salt, and cinnamon.

3. Add the melted butter, honey, and milk to the oat mixture, stirring until well combined.

4. Drop spoonfuls of the mixture onto the prepared baking sheet, flattening each one slightly to form small cakes.

5. Bake for 10-12 minutes, until the edges are golden brown.

6. Let the oat cakes cool on the baking sheet for a few minutes, then transfer to a wire rack to cool completely.

discussion questions

Exploring the life and contributions of Betsy Ross offers a rich tapestry of history, creativity, and resilience. Reflecting on her story can lead to deeper understanding and meaningful conversations. Here are some thought-provoking questions to consider as you think about Betsy's remarkable journey and the legacy she left behind.

1. What Motivated Betsy to Take on the Challenge of Making the First American Flag?

- Imagine being in Betsy's position when George Washington and other leaders asked her to create a flag for the new nation. What thoughts and emotions might she have experienced? Discuss the factors that might have motivated her to accept this important task despite the challenges she faced.

2. How Did Betsy's Quaker Faith Influence Her Actions and Decisions?

- Betsy Ross was raised in a Quaker family, and the values of her faith likely influenced her greatly. Think about how the principles of simplicity, honesty, and peace might have shaped her approach to her work and her interactions with others. How did her faith help her navigate the difficulties of the Revolutionary War?

3. What Role Did Creativity Play in Betsy's Life and Contributions?

- Creativity was a central aspect of Betsy's work, from her innovative approach to flag design to her skilled upholstery. Discuss how her creativity not only helped her succeed in her trade but also enabled her to make significant contributions to the American Revolution. How can creativity be a powerful tool in overcoming challenges?

4. What Can We Learn from Betsy's Perseverance Through Personal and Wartime Hardships?

- Betsy faced numerous hardships, including the loss of her husbands and the challenges of running a business during the war. Reflect on how she managed to persevere through these difficulties. What qualities and strategies did she use to stay strong and continue her work? How can we apply these lessons to our own lives?

5. How Did Betsy Ross's Contributions Extend Beyond the Creation of the Flag?

- While Betsy is best known for creating the first American flag, her impact went beyond this single achievement. Consider her role in the community, her support for the war effort, and her influence on future generations. Discuss the various ways Betsy contributed to the American cause and her lasting legacy.

6. Why Is the American Flag Such a Powerful

Symbol, and How Did Betsy's Flag Design Contribute to This?

- The American flag is a symbol of unity, freedom, and the ideals of the nation. Explore the significance of the flag's design, including the meaning of the stars and stripes. How did Betsy's choices in creating the flag contribute to its powerful symbolism? Why do symbols like the flag play an important role in national identity?

7. What Are Some Modern Parallels to Betsy Ross's Story of Innovation and Patriotism?

- Think about modern individuals or groups who have demonstrated similar qualities of innovation, resilience, and patriotism. How do their contributions reflect the values that Betsy embodied? Discuss how Betsy's story can inspire us to recognize and appreciate contemporary acts of courage and creativity.

8. How Can We Honor Betsy Ross's Legacy in Our Daily Lives?

- Betsy Ross's life and work offer many lessons that are still relevant today. Reflect on how we can honor her legacy through our own actions and choices. What can we do to embrace creativity, persevere through challenges, and contribute to our communities?

9. What Are Some Ways to Engage Younger Generations with Betsy Ross's Story?

- Betsy's story is not only a part of American history but also a source of inspiration for young people. Discuss creative and educational ways to introduce children to her life and contributions. How can we make history engaging and relevant for younger generations?

10. How Did Betsy's Personal Relationships Influence Her Work and Legacy?

- Betsy's relationships with her family, friends, and community played a significant role in her life. Consider how these connections supported her during difficult times and inspired her work. How do our relationships shape our own lives and contributions?

11. What Challenges Do You Think Betsy Faced as a Woman in Her Time, and How Did She Overcome Them?

- Reflect on the societal expectations and limitations placed on women in the 18th century. How did Betsy navigate these challenges to become a respected and influential figure? Discuss the progress made since then and the challenges that remain for women today.

12. What Does Betsy Ross's Story Teach Us About the Power of Individual Action in Shaping History?

- Betsy Ross's contributions remind us that individual actions can have a significant impact on history. Discuss examples from her life that illustrate this point. How can we each make a difference in our own communities and the world?

13. How Can We Use Betsy Ross's Story to Foster a Greater Appreciation for History and Heritage?

- Understanding and appreciating history is crucial for personal and societal growth. Discuss ways to use Betsy's story to encourage a deeper connection with history and heritage. How can learning about the past inspire us to build a better future?

14. What Are the Key Values and Principles We Can Learn from Betsy Ross's Life?

- Betsy Ross's life exemplifies several important values, such as perseverance, creativity, patriotism, and community spirit. Reflect on how these values are demonstrated in her actions and decisions.

How can we incorporate these principles into our own lives?

15. How Does Betsy Ross's Story Reflect the Broader Narrative of the American Revolution?

- Betsy's contributions are part of the larger story of the American Revolution. Discuss how her story fits into the broader context of the fight for independence. What does her experience tell us about the diverse efforts and sacrifices made by individuals during this pivotal time in history?

glossary

1. American Revolution

The American Revolution was a war fought between the thirteen American colonies and Great Britain from 1775 to 1783. The colonies sought independence from British rule, leading to the creation of the United States of America. The revolution was fueled by a desire for self-governance, economic freedom, and individual rights.

2. Continental Congress

The Continental Congress was a convention of delegates from the thirteen colonies that became the governing body during the American Revolution. It played a crucial role in coordinating the war effort, negotiating alliances, and drafting key documents such as the Declaration of Independence and the Articles of Confederation.

3. Declaration of Independence

The Declaration of Independence, adopted on July 4, 1776, was a statement issued by the Continental Congress declaring the colonies' independence from Great Britain. Written primarily by Thomas Jefferson, it outlined the colonies' grievances against King George III and articulated the principles of individual liberty and government by consent.

4. Patriots

Patriots were American colonists who supported independence from Great Britain. They believed in the right to self-governance and fought against British control during the American Revolution. Betsy Ross and many others who contributed to the cause of independence were considered patriots.

5. Quakers

Quakers, or the Religious Society of Friends, are a Christian group known for their commitment to peace, simplicity, and equality. Betsy Ross was raised in a Quaker family, and her values and actions were influenced by her Quaker upbringing. Quakers played various roles during the American Revolution, often advocating for nonviolence and humanitarian principles.

6. Upholsterer

An upholsterer is a craftsperson who works with furniture, particularly in covering and padding items such as chairs and sofas. Betsy Ross was an upholsterer, a skill that proved crucial when she was asked to create the first American flag. Her expertise in sewing and fabric work made her well-suited for this important task.

7. Flag

A flag is a piece of fabric with a distinctive design used as a symbol, signaling device, or decoration. The American flag, also known as the Stars and Stripes, was designed by Betsy Ross and has become a powerful symbol of the United States. It represents the nation's ideals of freedom, unity, and justice.

8. Thirteen Colonies

The thirteen colonies were British colonies on the east coast of North America that declared independence in 1776. These colonies formed the original United States. The colonies included Delaware, Pennsylvania, New Jersey, Georgia, Connecticut, Massachusetts Bay, Maryland, South Carolina, New Hampshire, Virginia, New York, North Carolina, and Rhode Island and Providence Plantations.

9. Independence Hall

Independence Hall is a historic building in Philadelphia, Pennsylvania, where both the Declaration of Independence and the United States Constitution were debated and adopted. It is an iconic symbol of American democracy and the struggle for independence. The building was originally the Pennsylvania State House.

10. Liberty Bell

The Liberty Bell is an iconic symbol of American independence and freedom. Originally housed in the Pennsylvania State House (now Independence Hall), it was rung to mark important events and announcements. The bell is famously inscribed with the words "Proclaim Liberty Throughout All the Land Unto All the Inhabitants Thereof."

11. Continental Army

The Continental Army was the unified military force established by the Continental Congress to fight against British forces during the American Revolution. Led by General George Washington, the Continental Army played a crucial role in securing American independence. It was comprised of soldiers from all thirteen colonies.

12. Betsy Ross House

The Betsy Ross House is a historic house in Philadelphia, Pennsylvania, where Betsy Ross is believed to have lived and sewn the first American flag. The house is now a museum dedicated to her life and contributions. Visitors can explore the house and learn about Betsy's role in American history.

13. Symbolism

Symbolism refers to the use of symbols to represent ideas or qualities. The American flag, with its stars and stripes, is rich in symbolism. Each element of the flag, such as the thirteen stripes representing the original colonies and the stars representing the states, carries significant meaning related to the nation's history and values.

14. George Washington

George Washington was the commander-in-chief of the Continental Army during the American Revolution and later became the first President of the United States. He played a pivotal role in the fight for independence and in the early years of the new nation. Washington's leadership and vision were instrumental in shaping the United States.

15. Philadelphia

Philadelphia is a historic city in Pennsylvania that played a central role in the American Revolution. It was the meeting place of the Continental Congress and the site where the Declaration of Independence was adopted. Philadelphia is home to many significant landmarks, including Independence Hall and the Betsy Ross House.

16. Treaty of Paris (1783)

The Treaty of Paris, signed in 1783, officially ended the American Revolutionary War. The treaty recognized the independence of the United States and established the boundaries of the new nation. It was a significant milestone in the creation of the United States and the conclusion of the struggle for independence.

17. Colonial

The term "colonial" refers to the period of American history when the thirteen colonies were under British rule. The colonial era includes the time from the founding of the first colonies in the early 1600s to the start of the American Revolution in the late 1700s. This period was marked by the development of colonial society and increasing tensions with Great Britain.

18. Revolutionary War

The Revolutionary War, also known as the American War of Independence, was the conflict between the American colonies and Great Britain from 1775 to 1783. The war resulted in the colonies gaining their independence and forming the United States. It was characterized by significant battles, strategic alliances, and the determination of the American people.

19. Liberty

Liberty is the state of being free from oppressive

restrictions imposed by authority on one's way of life, behavior, or political views. The quest for liberty was a driving force behind the American Revolution, as the colonists sought freedom from British rule and the ability to govern themselves.

20. Sewing

Sewing is the craft of fastening or attaching objects using stitches made with a needle and thread. Betsy Ross's expertise in sewing was crucial in her creation of the first American flag. Sewing was a vital skill in the 18th century, used for making and repairing clothing, household items, and other necessities.

bibliography

Websites

1. Betsy Ross House (https://www.betsyrosshouse.org)
- The official website of the Betsy Ross House offers a wealth of information about Betsy Ross's life, the history of the American flag, and the historic site itself. Virtual tours, educational resources, and event information are available, making it a valuable resource for both students and educators.

2. National Archives (https://www.archives.gov)
- The National Archives website provides access to a vast collection of historical documents, including those related to the American Revolution. It's a great place to explore primary sources and gain a deeper understanding of the historical context.

3. Smithsonian National Museum of American History (https://americanhistory.si.edu)
- The Smithsonian's National Museum of American History website offers extensive resources on American history, including exhibits on the American Revolution and the American flag. Interactive features and educational materials make it an engaging site for learners of all ages.

4. Library of Congress (https://www.loc.gov)
- The Library of Congress website provides access to an extensive collection of historical documents, photographs, and multimedia resources. It's an excellent resource for

researching American history and exploring primary sources.

5. History Channel (https://www.history.com)
- The History Channel's website features articles, videos, and educational resources on a wide range of historical topics, including the American Revolution and Betsy Ross. It's a great place to find engaging content that complements traditional study materials.

6. PBS LearningMedia (https://www.pbslearningmedia.org)
- PBS LearningMedia offers a variety of educational resources, including videos, lesson plans, and interactive activities related to American history. It's a valuable tool for teachers and students looking for high-quality, multimedia content.

www.ingramcontent.com/pod-product-compliance
Lightning Source LLC
Chambersburg PA
CBHW051213160726
47994CB00002B/589